This book
belongs to:

____

"With each conscious breath, we connect with the natural rhythm of the Earth."

"Nature whispers her wisdom to
those who stop to listen."

"Take a moment to listen to the rustle
of waves and the song of whales -
nature's symphony is a mindful
meditation in itself."

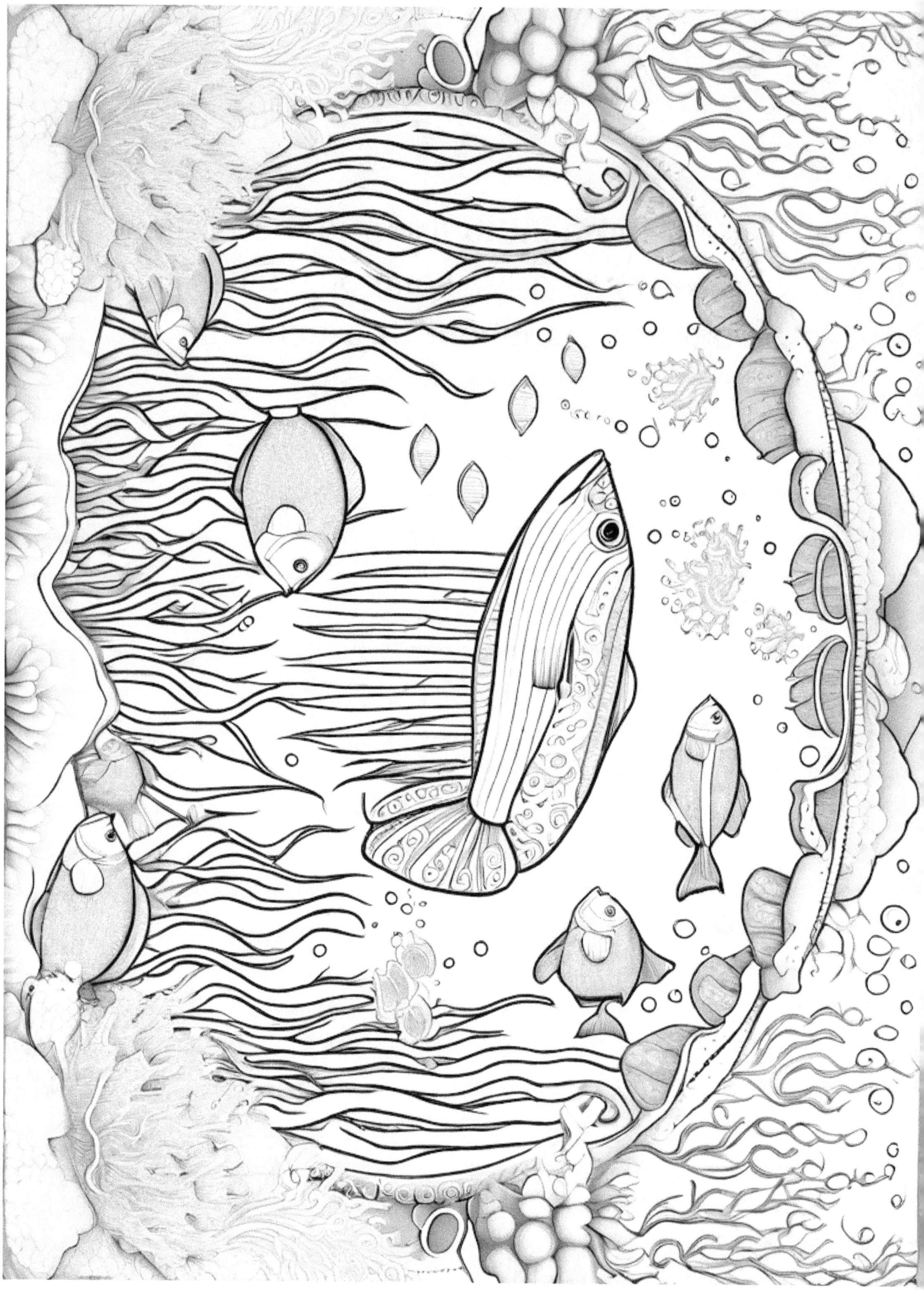

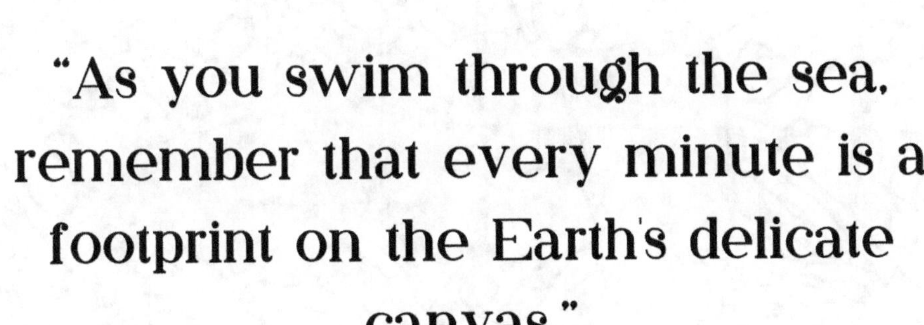

"As you swim through the sea,
remember that every minute is a
footprint on the Earth's delicate
canvas."

"Mindfulness teaches us to appreciate the beauty of a single fish, reminding us of the intricate web of life it represents."

"Preserving nature not as a chore, but as an act of self-preservation for our own well-being."

"Recycle not only materials, but also thoughts, transforming waste into ecologically correct actions."

"The stillness of a mountain lake reflects the serenity of a conscious mind."

"Practice gratitude for the clean air you breathe, as every breath connects you to the world."

"When you save a tree, you are saving a piece of history, a home to countless creatures and a source of inspiration for mindfulness."

"Inhale the smell of fresh rain, exhale stress toxins – nature therapy is always open."

———

"Let your actions in nature conservation be guided by a heart full of mindfulness, compassion and love for our planet."

"Meditate on the beauty of the earth and you will find mindfulness in every leaf and stream."

"An attentive heart beats in harmony
with the planet."

"By protecting nature, we nurture
our own well-being."

"The present moment and the beauty
of nature are one."

"Mindfulness flourishes where nature thrives."

"Preserve the planet, preserve its peace."

"With every step in nature, we get closer
to mindfulness."

———————————

"Caring for the environme
nt is an act of
self-care for our souls."

"Nature whispers her wisdom
to those who stop to listen."

"Nature imparts her wisdom to those
who stop to listen."

"The present moment and the beauty of
nature are intertwined."

"The preservation of nature is a conscious act of gratitude for the world around us."

____

"In the stillness of nature, we fin
d the stillness of mindfulness."

"Each tree planted is a step towards conservation and inner peace."

"Mindfulness and nature are two wings
of the same spiritual journey."

"The art of mindfulness begins with apprec iating the art of nature."

"Caring for the environment is a profound form
of self-care."

"In the embrace of nature, we discover
our truest selves."

""Mindfulness is the lens through which
we realize the beauty of our planet."

"Nature reminds us to be present, to breathe and to value the Earth."

"Our relationship with nature reflects our
relationship with ourselves;
nurture both with care."

____

"In the stillness of nature, mindfulness
becomes a gentle breeze."

"As we protect the environment,
we safeguard our own inner serenity."

———————————

"Mindfulness blooms like wildflowers
in the meadows of the present moment."

"As we protect the environment,
we safeguard our own inner serenity."

"Mindfulness extends to the vastness
of the ocean, urging us to protect its wonders."

"The rhythm of the waves teaches
us the art of being in the present moment."

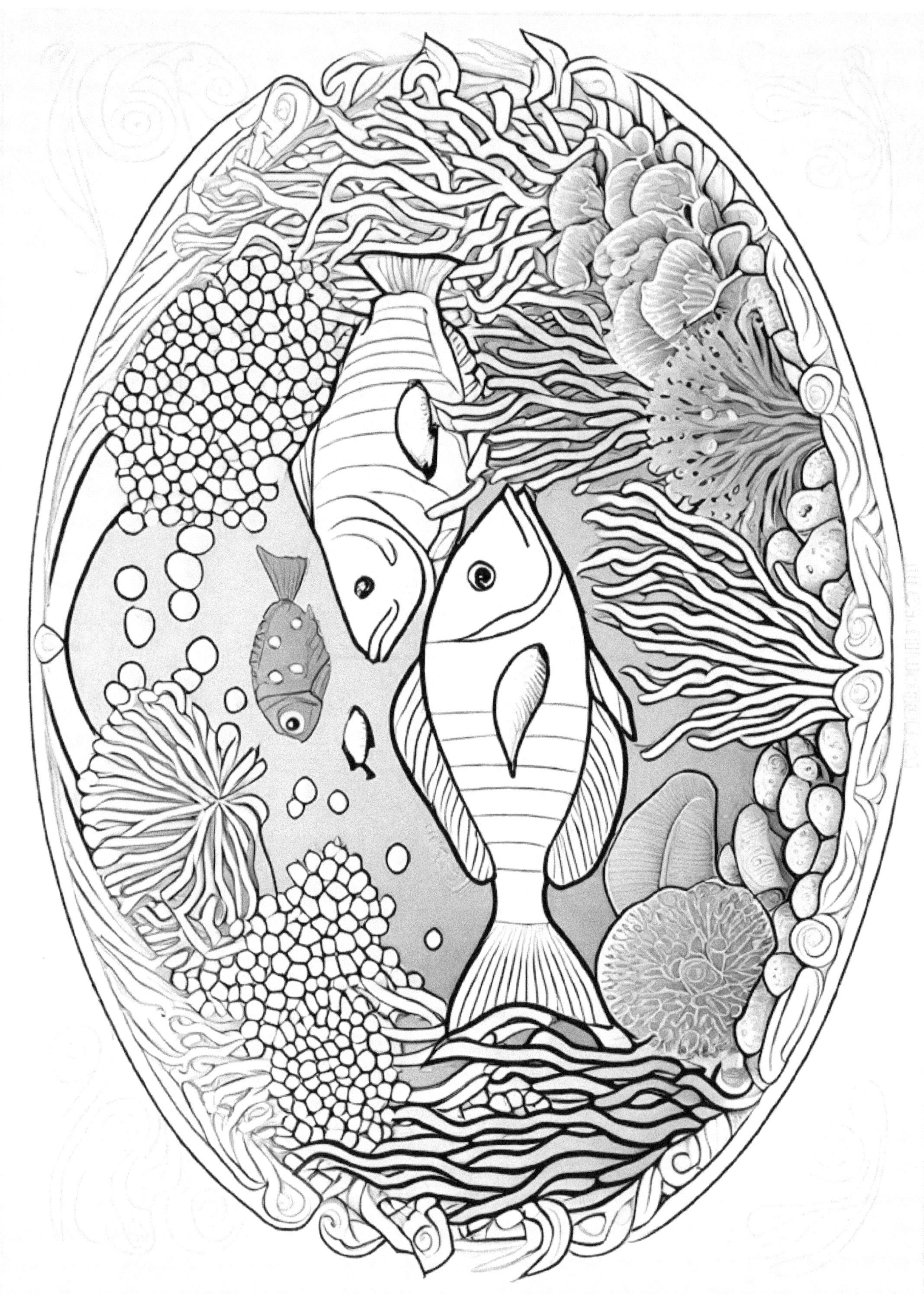

"Every piece of plastic we remove from
the ocean is a step towards
environmental awareness."

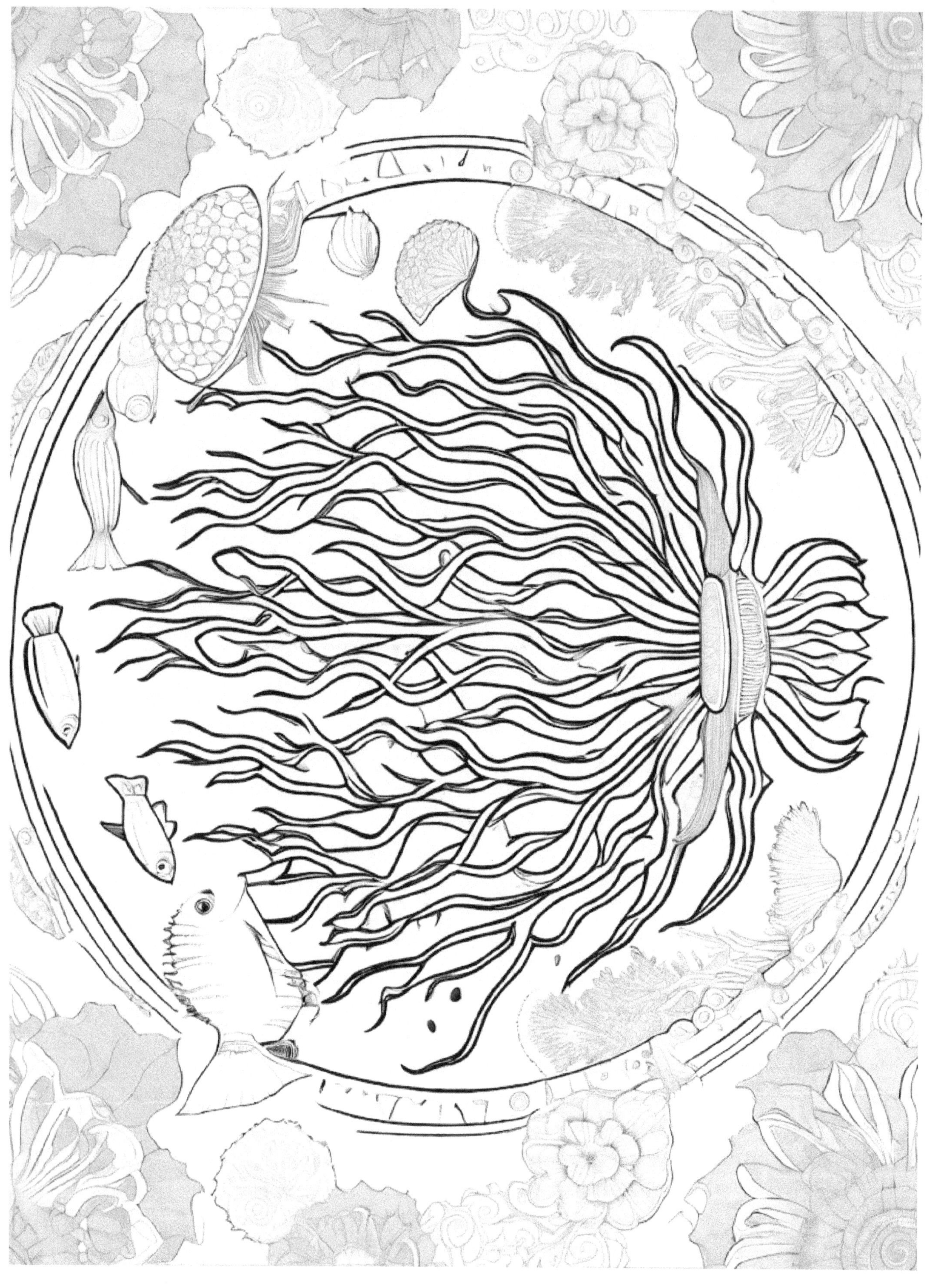

"Safeguarding the ocean is an act of
preserving the beating
heart of the Earth."

"In the depths of the ocean, we find a
wonderful world worth preserving."

"As we immerse ourselves in the beauty
of the ocean, we learn the
value of conservation."

"Mindfulness at sea means understanding
our role in the delicate balance
of marine life."

———————

"The health of our oceans
is a reflection of our collective
attention."

Songs of Conscious Conservation: Melody of Nature

Beneath the sky's vast tapestry, we stand,
In mindful moments, hand in hand,
With nature's beauty, pure and free,
A tranquil world, our hearts decree.

In whispers of the leaves and breeze,
We find our souls at perfect ease,
With every breath, we're intertwined,
With Earth's embrace, a love defined.

The ocean's waves, they rise and fall,
A mindful dance, a sacred call,
To care for waters, deep and wide,
Where life's abundant, deep inside.

In mindful gaze, we watch the sea,
Its mysteries and majesty,
A symphony of life so grand,
In nature's palm, we understand.

With mindful steps on sandy shores,
We feel the Earth, our hearts implore,
To preserve every living part,
In unity, we heal the heart.

With every choice, a ripple flows,
Through nature's realms, its beauty shows,
In mindfulness, we find the key,
To protect Earth's vast, harmonious sea.

So let us vow, in mindful grace,
To cherish nature's sacred space,
In every breath and gentle sway,
Preservation guides our way.